LOCALS
GUIDE BOOK

GUILIN
YANGSHUO
XINGPING
+EXTRA'S

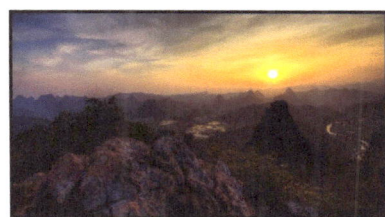

MOON HILL

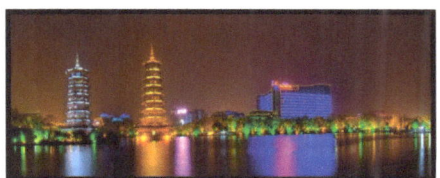

GUILIN

16 VIEWPOINTS

EASY TO USE GUIDE BOOK
GUIDED BY THE USE OF MAPS,
PICTURES AND INSTRUCTIONS
TO GET YOU TO THOSE PLACES

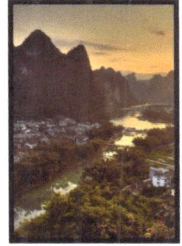

XINGPING

WWW.ANOTHERDAYATTHEOFFICE.ORG

CONTENTS

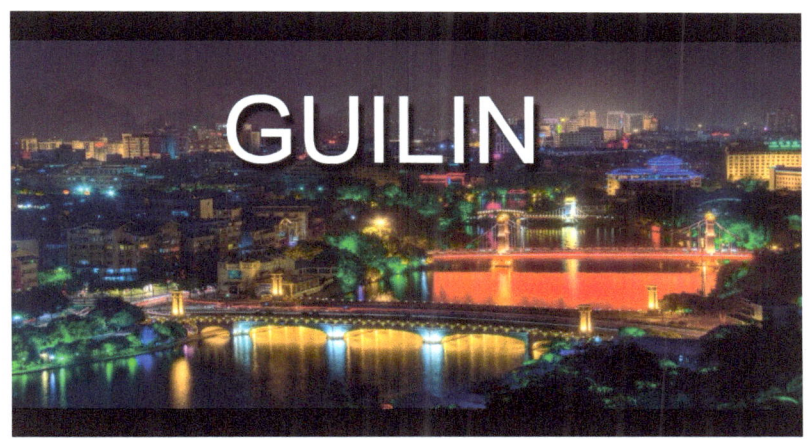

GUILIN

HIDDEN VIEWPOINT

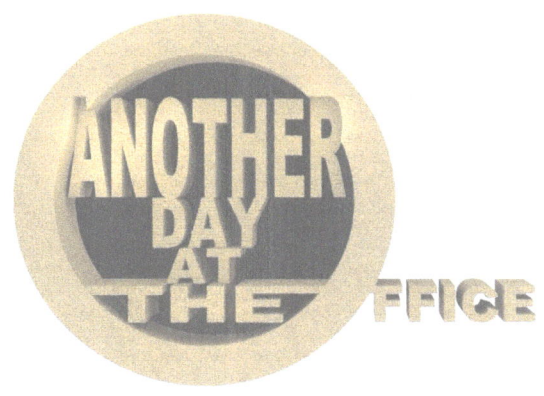

www.anotherdayattheoffice.org

0b

2 RIVERS AND FOUR LAKES TOUR:

Start : DEICAI HILL   .叠彩山

End : SHAN LAKE
            SUN AND MOON PAGODAS

Duration:1/3Hr

How to get there:by taxi
show deicai hill to taxi driver .叠彩山

When: day time or evening

Shan lake/sun and moon pagoda

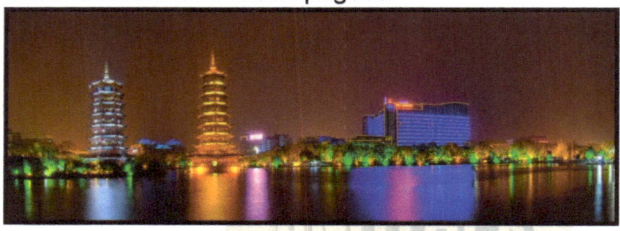

Mulonglake from deicai hill

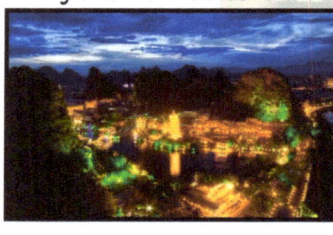

0c

MAP OF GUILIN .桂林

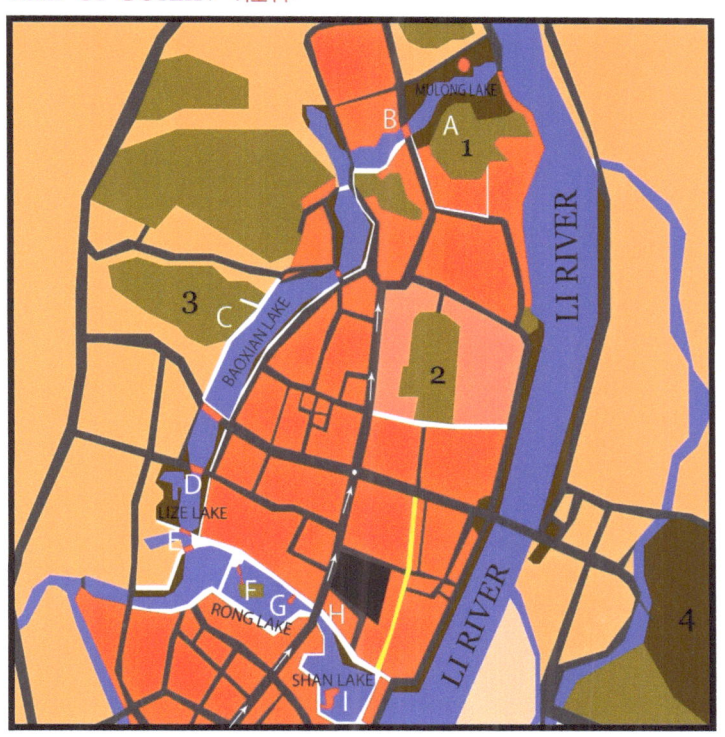

1 DIECAI HILL .叠彩山
2 SOLITARY BEAUTY PEAK .独秀峰
3 LIUMA HILL(HIDDEN VIEWPOINT)
4 SEVEN STAR CAVE PARK .七星岩公园

■ DIFFERENT VIEWPOINTS DURING YOUR ROUTE
▢ YOUR ROUTE   ■ WATER/LI-RIVER
➡ MAIN STREET   ▬ SHOPPING STREET
▬ CITY SQUARE(GLASS PYRAMIDES)

1

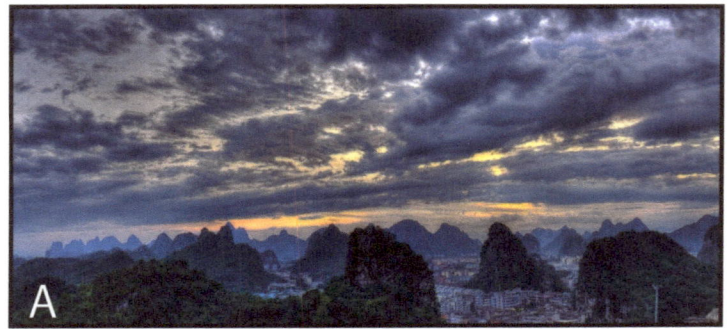

SUNSET FROM DIECAI HILL

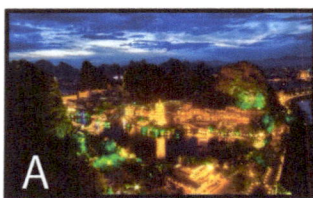

NIGHT VIEW ON MULONG LAKE AND TOWER
FROM DIECAI HILL

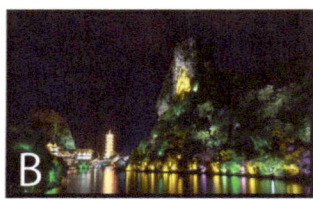

NIGHT VIEW ON MULONG LAKE AND TOWER
FROM BRIDGE/START

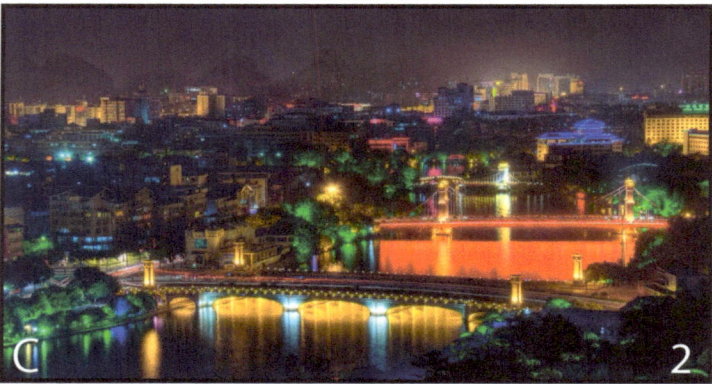

HIDDEN VIEWPOINT

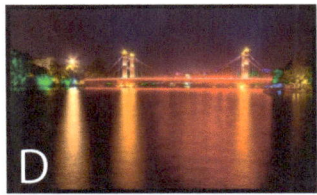

LIZE BRIDGE AT LIZE LAKE

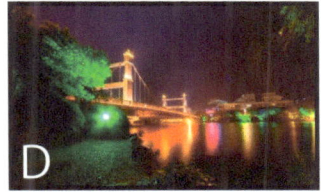

LIZE BRIDGE AT LIZE LAKE

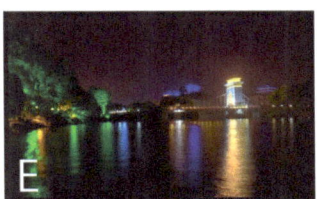

YINGBING BRIDGE AT RONG LAKE

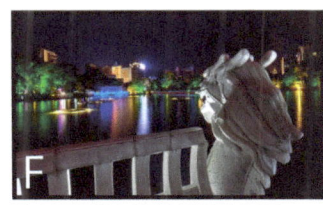

PLATFORM AT RONG LAKE

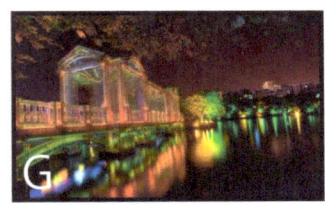

GLASS BRIDGE AT RONG LAKE

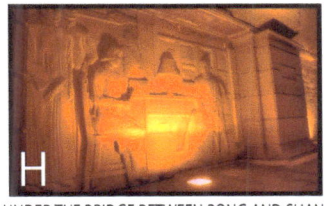

UNDER THE BRIDGE BETWEEN RONG AND SHAN

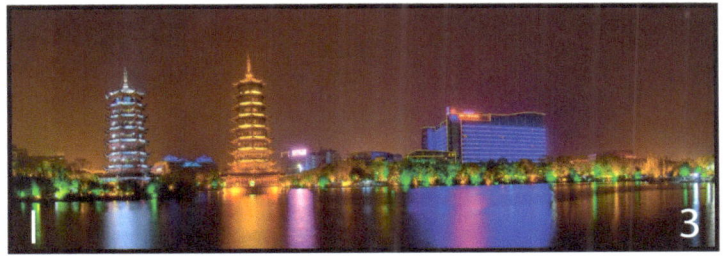

SUN AND MOON PAGODAS AT SHAN LAKE

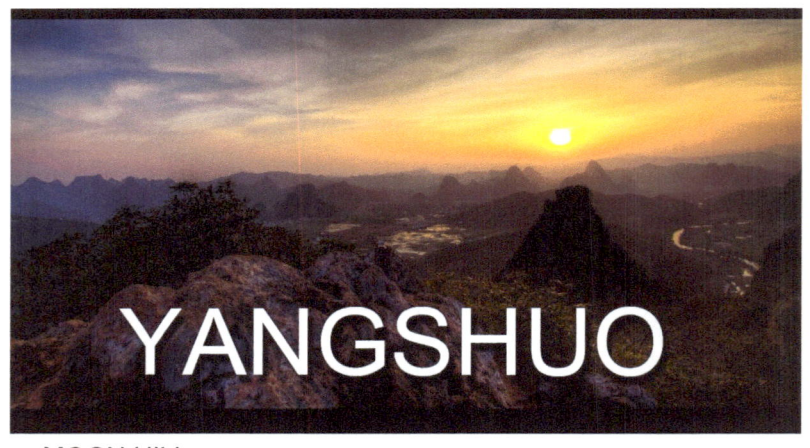

YANGSHUO

MOON HILL

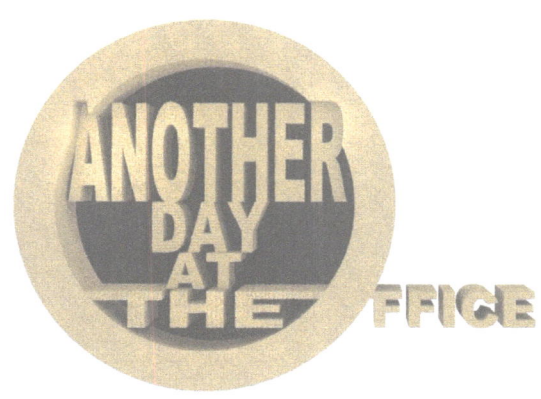

www.anotherdayattheoffice.org

3a

MAP OF YANGSHUO.阳朔

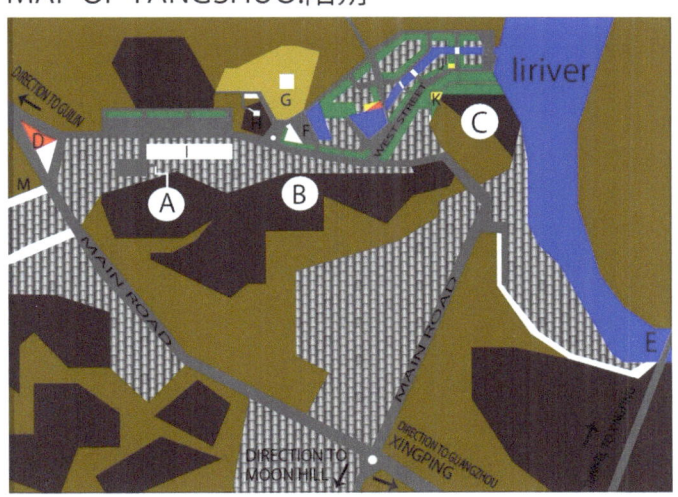

A.TV TOWER
B.TELECOM TOWER
C.GREEN LOTUS PEAK
D.GAS STATION
E.YANGSHUO BRIDGE
F. PARKING LOT
G.YANGSHUO PARK
H.PAGODA INSIDE PARK
I.FRUIT AND MEAT MARKET

VEGETATION
KARST MOUNTAINS
ASPHALT ROADS
YANGSHUO PARK
WATER
TOWN HOUSES AND SHOPS
MACDONALDS
DIFFERENT HOSTELS AND BAR
HOUSES AROUND YANGSHUO
ROUNDABOUT
CYCLING TRAIL

M.CYCLING TRAIL TO YULONG RIVER,MOON HILL

4

阳朔

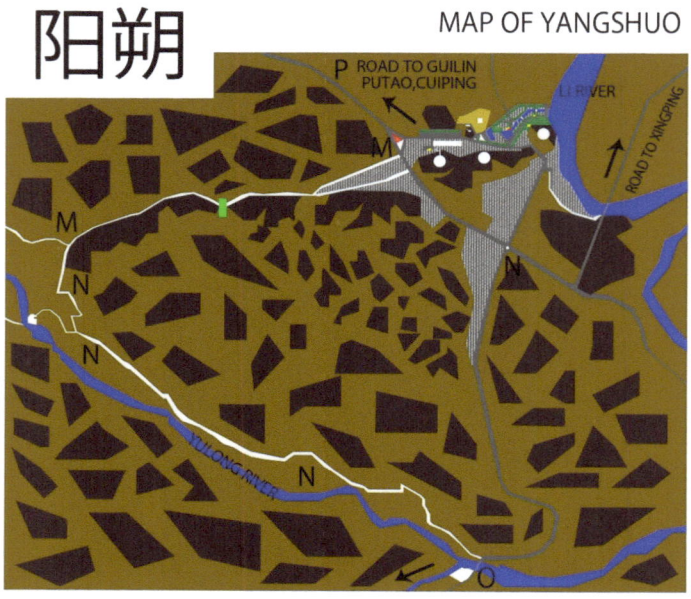

M. CYCLING TRAIL TO DRAGON BRIDGE ,YULONG RIVER
N. CYCLING TRAIL TO MOON HILL
O. MAIN ROAD TO MOON HILL,SILVER CAVE
P. MAIN ROAD TO GUILIN,CUIPING,PUTAO
▮. SQUARE GATE

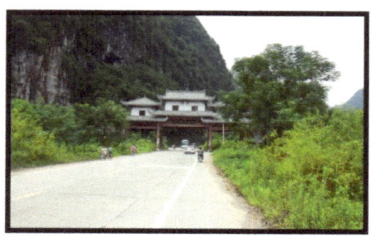

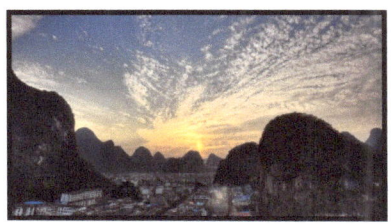

SMALL PAGODA

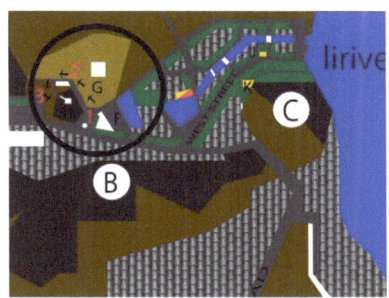

G. YANGSHUO PARK
F. PARKING LOT
H. SMALL PAGODA VIEWPOINT

1. ENTER YANGSHUO PARK
FOLLOW THE PATH
AT YOUR LEFT CARNIVAL RIDES
2. TURN LEFT AFTER THE CARNIVAL RIDES
WALK +/- 300M AND TURN LEFT AGAIN
3. FOLLOW THIS PATH FOR 100M
AT YOUR LEFT THERE'S STAIRS GOING UP

6

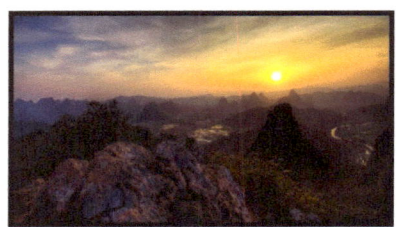

MOON HILL

阳朔

MAP OF YANGSHUO

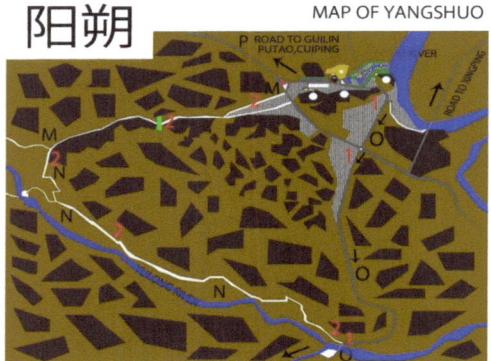

M. CYCLING TRAIL TO DRAGON BRIDGE ,YULONG RIVER
N. CYCLING TRAIL TO MOON HILL
O. MAIN ROAD TO MOON HILL,SILVER CAVE
P. MAIN ROAD TO GUILIN,CUIPING,PUTAO
▮. SQUARE GATE

1. ROUTE TO MOON HILL/MAIN ROAD.NR1

START IN THE TOWN CENTER DIRECTION XINGPING
AT THE ROUNDABOUT GO STRAIGHT
FOLLOW THE ROAD,THEN CROSS THE BRIDGE AT YULONG RIVER
KEEP FOLLOWING THE ROAD FOR +/- 10 MIN
THEN AT YOU'RE RIGHT THE ENTRANCE OFF MOON HILL

2. ROUTE TO MOON HILL/CYCLING TRAIL.NR2

START IN THE TOWN CENTER DIRECTION GUILIN
BEFORE THE GAS STATION,TURN LEFT AND CROSS THE ROAD
FOLLOW THE ROAD,YOU GONNA CROSS A SQUARE GATE
KEEP GOING STRAIGHT AND AT THE INTERSECTION TURN LEFT,FOLLOW THE PATH NEXT TO THE RIVER
UNTILL THE BRIDGE AT YULONG RIVER AND CROSS THE RIVER,GO STRAIGHT FOR +/- 10 MIN
THEN AT YOU'RE RIGHT MOON HILL

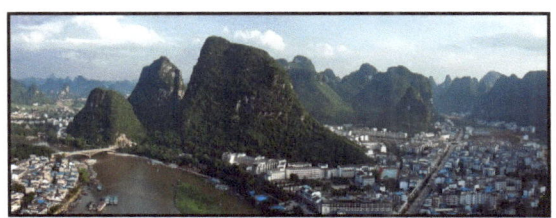

GREEN LOTUS PEAK

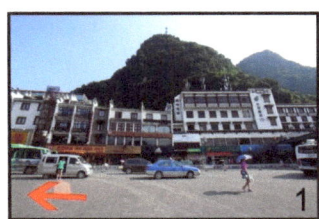

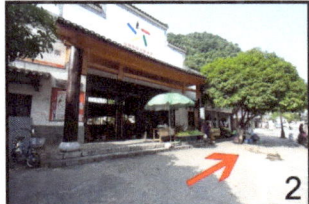

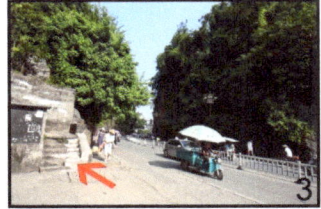

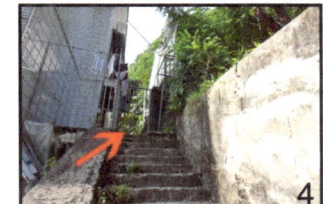

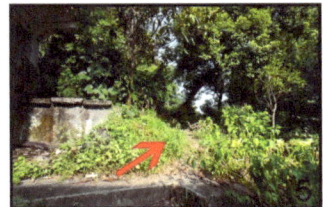

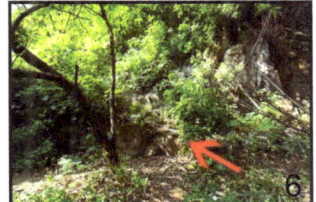

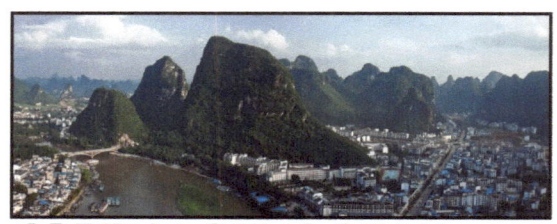

GREEN LOTUS PEAK

1. AT THE BEGINNING OF WEST STREET,
   GO LEFT,IN FRONT TELECOM TOWER

2. GO STRAIGHT,AT YOUR LEFT INDOOR SPORT

3. GET THE STAIRS AT YOUR LEFT

4. GET UP THESE STAIRS AND THEN RIGHT
5. FOLLOW THIS PATH
6. AT YOUR LEFT,THERES A PATH GOING UP
7.AT THE TOP GO RIGHT FOR REAL SUMMIT

BE WARNED,AFTER RAIN,VERY DANGEROUS PATH

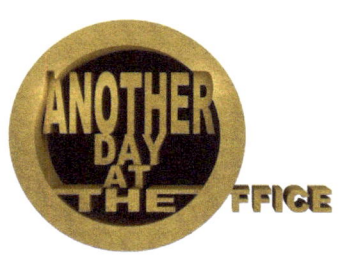

8a

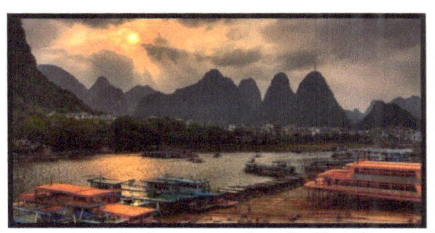

YANGSHUO BRIDGE

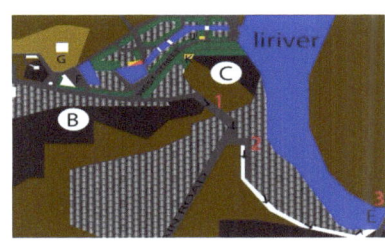

B.TELECOM TOWER
C.GREEN LOTUS PEAK
E.YANGSHUO BRIDGE
F.BUS STATION YANGSHUO
G.YANGSHUO PARK

I.FRUIT AND MEAT MARKEY
J.CAFE CHINA
K.MONKEY JANE YOUTH HOSTEL
L.HOW FLOWERS HOSTEL

1. START IN THE CITY CENTER DIRECTION XINGPING
2.TAKE THE SMALL ROAD NEXT TO THE LI RIVER
3.WALK 10 MIN ,THEN YOU GET AT YANGSHUO BRIDGE

9

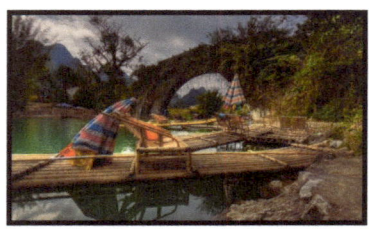

YULONG RIVER AND BRIDGES

阳朔

MAP OF YANGSHUO

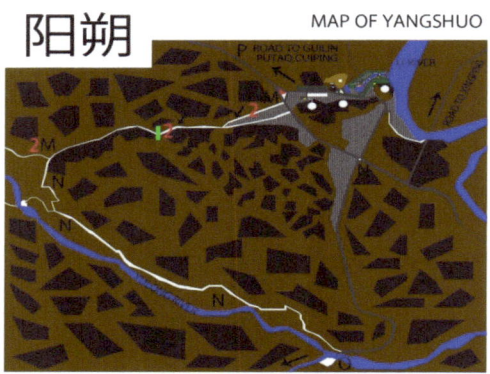

M. CYCLING TRAIL TO DRAGON BRIDGE ,YULONG RIVER
N. CYCLING TRAIL TO MOON HILL
O. MAIN ROAD TO MOON HILL,SILVER CAVE
P. MAIN ROAD TO GUILIN,CUIPING,PUTAO
. SQUARE GATE

2. ROUTE TO YULONG RIVER AND BRIDGES

START IN THE TOWN CENTER DIRECTION GUILIN
BEFORE THE GAS STATION,TURN LEFT AND CROSS THE ROAD
FOLLOW THE ROAD,YOU GONNA CROSS A SQUARE GATE
KEEP GOING STRAIGHT AND AT THE INTERSECTION TURN RIGHT
FOLLOW THE PATH NEXT TO THE RIVER,DIIFERENT BRIDGES ON THE WAY
FULI BRIDGE,YULONG BRIDGE(dragon bridge)

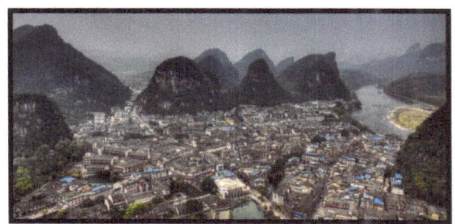

TV TOWER

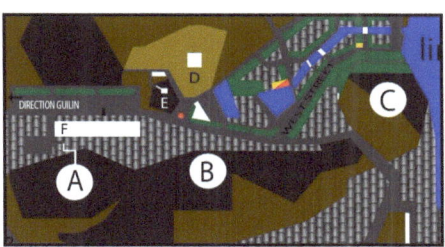

A.TV TOWER
B.TELECOM TOWER
C.GREEN LOTUS PEAK
D.YANGSHUO PARK
E.PAGODA VIEWPOINT
F.POSTAL SAVINGS
  BANK OF CHINA
.ROUNDABOUT

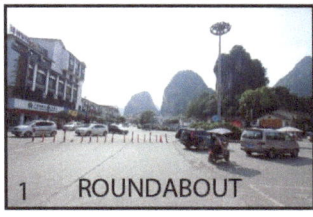

1 ROUNDABOUT

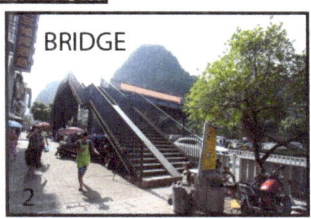

BRIDGE

2

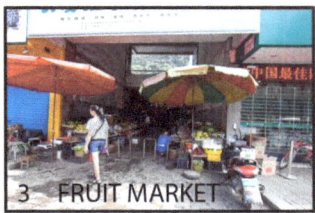

3 FRUIT MARKET

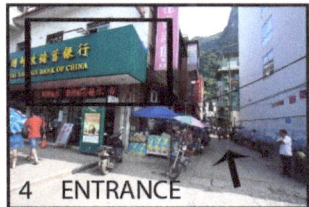

4 ENTRANCE

11

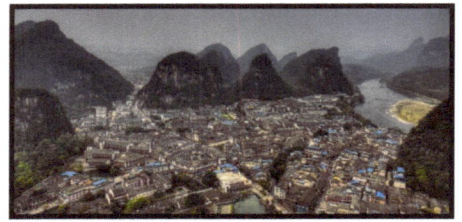

TV TOWER

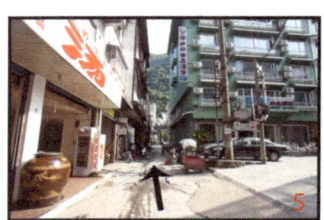

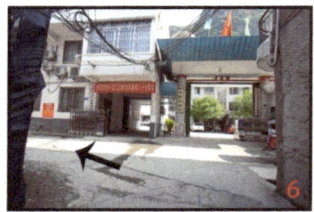

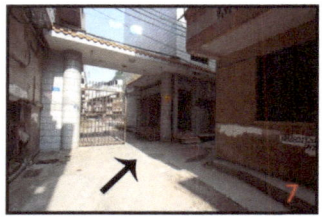

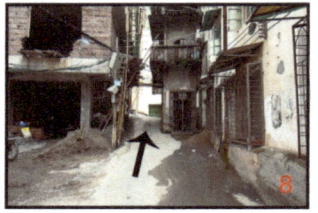

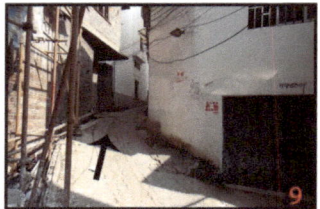

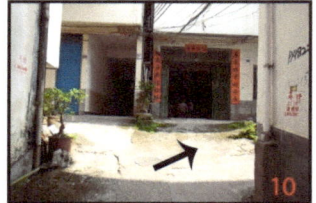

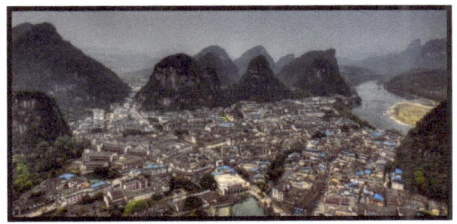

TV TOWER

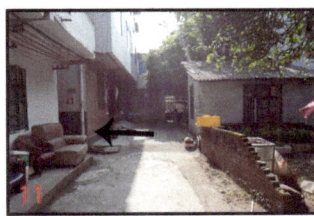

11

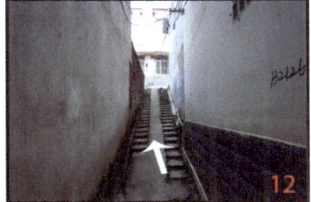

12

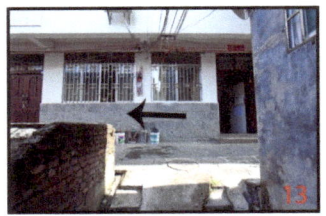

13

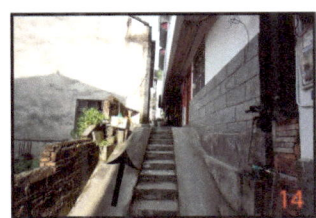

14

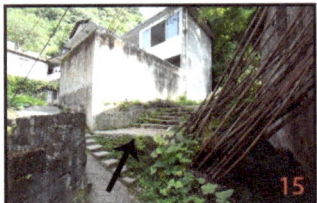

15

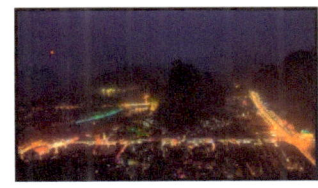

BACKSIDE VIEW/NIGHT

13

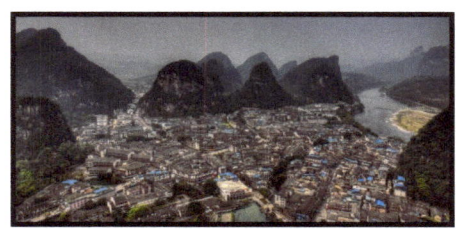

TV TOWER

1. START AT THE ROUNDABOUT,HEADING TOWARDS GUILIN
2. BRIDGE AT YOUR RIGHT
3. FRUIT MARKET AT YOUR LEFT
4. POSTAL SAVINGS BANK AT YOUR LEFT/ENTRANCE
5. FOLLOW THIS ALLEY STRAIGHT
6. TURN LEFT AT THE END OF THE ALLEY
7. TURN RIGHT AT THE GATE
8. GO STRAIGHT
9. GO LEFT,UPHILL
10. GO RIGHT
11. TAKE THIS SMALL ALLEY TO THE LEFT
12. STRAIGHT TO THIS ALLEY
13. GO LEFT AFTER THIS SMALL ALLEY
14. FOLLOW THIS PATH UP
15. GET THE STAIRS AT YOUR RIGHT

XINGPING

LAOZHAI HILL

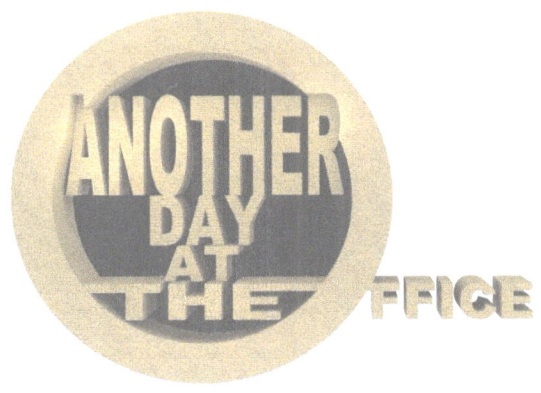

www.anotherdayattheoffice.org

14a

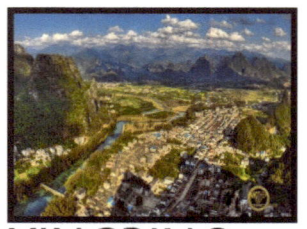

XINGPING

THE ANCIENT TOWN OF XINGPING=兴坪古⊠

THE HIDDEN PEARL,25KM FROM YANGSHUO
BUILD IN 625 ,MING AND XING DYNASTY

HOW TO GET THERE:

by local bus:at yangshuo bus station to xingping around 7 rmb.p/p.45min
by bamboo raft from guilin:bus to yangdi and then to xingping.around 60rmb/p4p
by bamboo raft from yangshuo:bamboo raft to xingping.around 55rmb/p4p

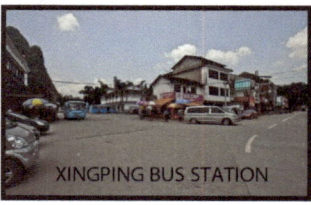

XINGPING BUS STATION

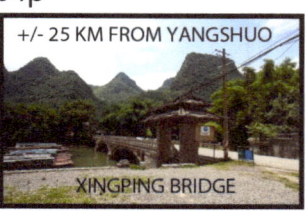

+/- 25 KM FROM YANGSHUO

XINGPING BRIDGE

BE WARNED

BETTER TO STAY FOR A FEW DAYS,PHOTOGRAPHERS PARADISE

MAP OF XINGPING. 兴坪

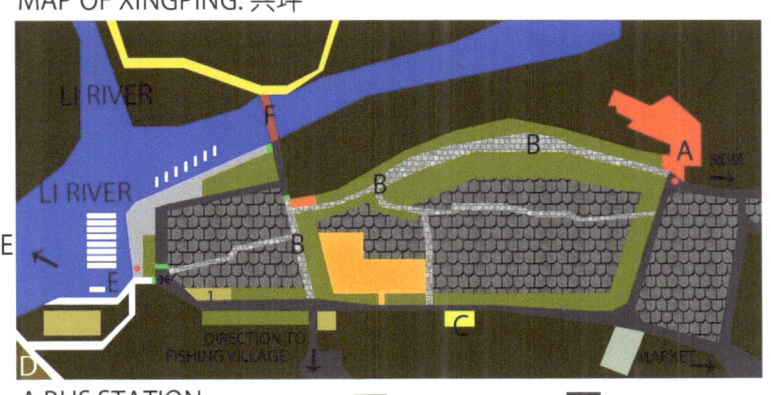

A.BUS STATION
B.OLD STREET/COBBLESTONE
C.BIG SUPERMARKET
D.LOAZHAI HILL
E.SMALL FERRY TO CROSS LI RIVER
F.BRIDGE

■ VEGETATION AND TREES	■ ASPHALT ROAD
■ SHOPS AND RESTAURANTS	■ CYCLING/HIKING TRAIL
■ OLD PLACE RESTAURANT	■ SCHOOL
■ 1.OLD PLACE HOSTEL	■ OLD PLACE HOSTEL AND HOTELS
■ ✳ ROUND AND SQUARE GATE	■ GATES
■ XINGPING PIER/RAFT	■ GOLF CAR PARKING
▨ OLD STREET/COBBLESTONE	▨ LOCAL HOUSES ROOF

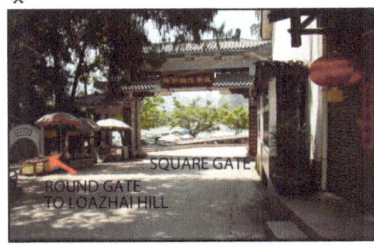

ROUND GATE
TO LOAZHAI HILL
SQUARE GATE

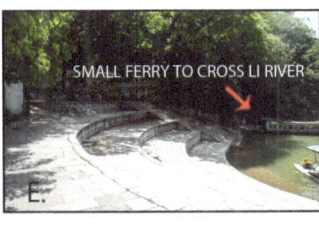

SMALL FERRY TO CROSS LI RIVER

E.

15a

MAP OF XINGPING.兴坪

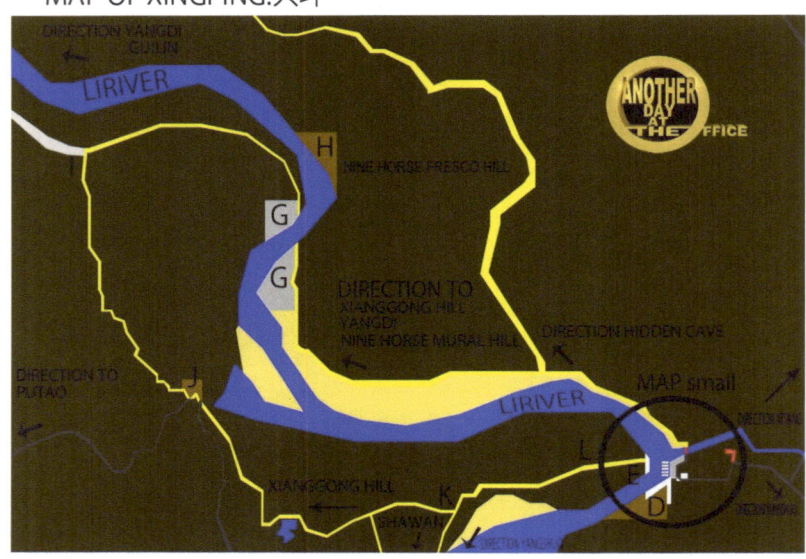

G. FERRY TO CROSS RIVER
H. NINE HORSE MURAL HILL
I. HIKING TRAIL TO YANGDI
J. XIANGGONG HILL
K. INTERSECTION TO SHAWAN AND XIANGGONG HILL
L. ROAD TO XIANGGONG,SHAWAN

- CYCLING/HIKING TRAIL
- VEGETATION AND TREES
- HIKING TRAIL YANGDI
- SAND BANKS
- NINE HORSE FRESCO HILL
- POND AND LI RIVER
- CONCRETE SMALL ROAD

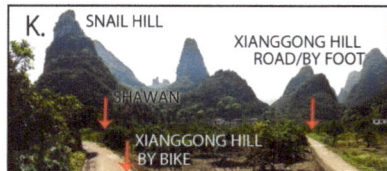

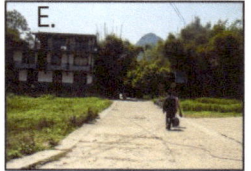

15b

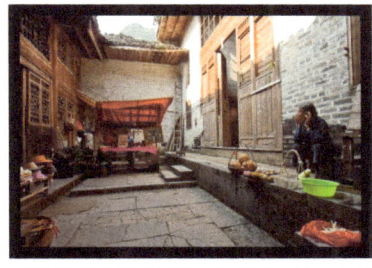

FISHING
VILLAGE

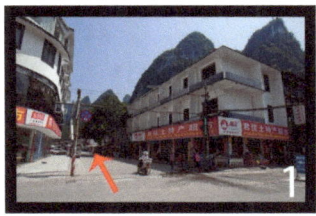

1

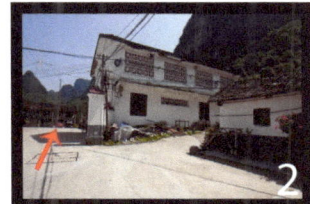

2

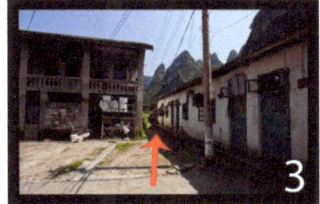

3

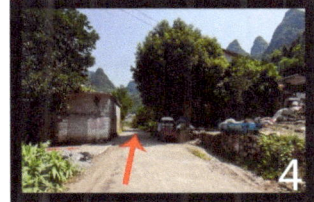

4

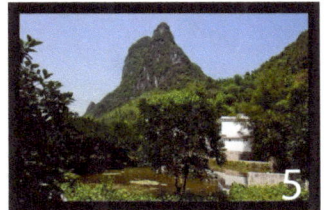

5

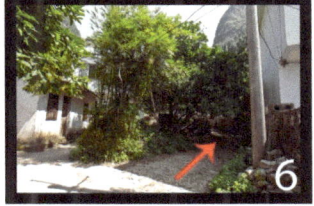

6

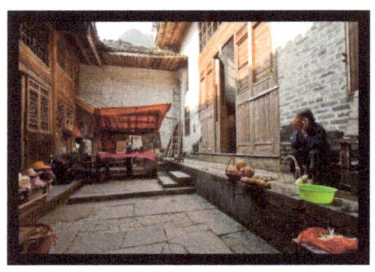

FISHING
VILLAGE

1. follow this way at the crossroad
沿着十字路口的这条街走

2. follow the way at the local houses
然后沿着这栋房子左侧的路走下去

3. follow the way between the houses
再穿过这两座房子中间走到后面

4. follow the road straight
沿着此路一直往前走

5. then at your left,there will be a pond
走到头会看到一个小池塘

follow the way straight,and then at your right

6. the path goes up 此时沿着右手边一条
窄窄的小路走上去
水泥路上山

17

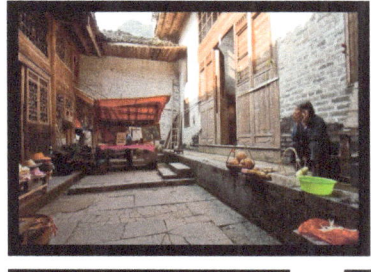

FISHING
VILLAGE

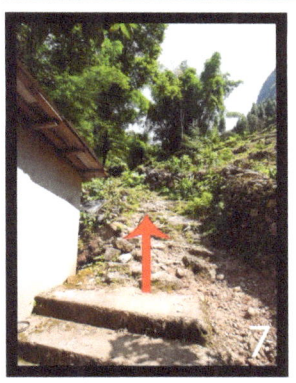

7

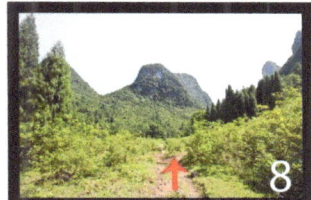

8

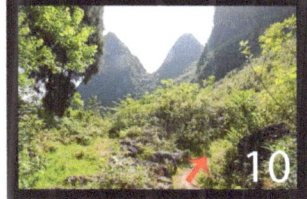

10

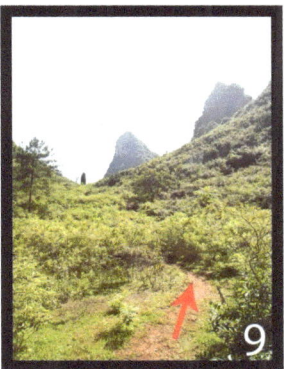

9

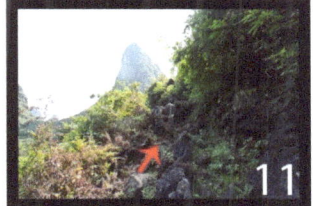

11

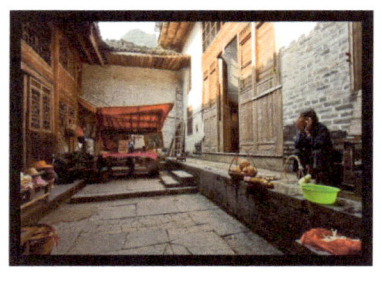

FISHING
VILLAGE

7. follow this path up
然后一直往上走

8. untill the plateau,keep right
走到高处的平地，注意要走向右边

9. then follow the way up,to the crossing
接着再沿着小路往上走一段，
会看到分叉口

10. at the crossing,go right
在此又要选右手的小路走

11. follow the path,pass the rocks
沿着小路往前走，翻过一个石堆

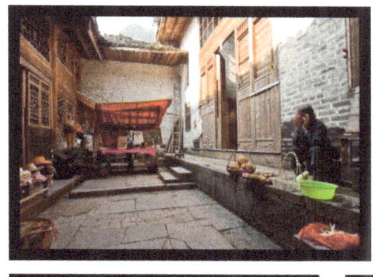

FISHING
VILLAGE

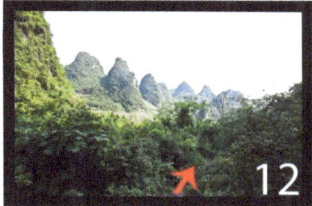

12

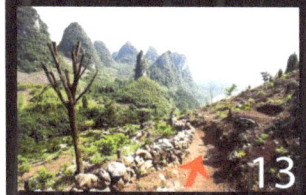

13

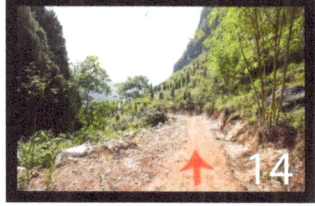

14

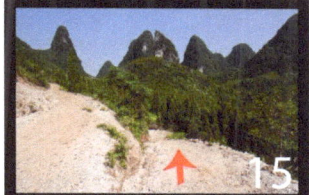

15

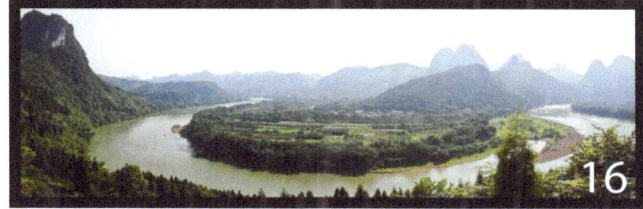

16

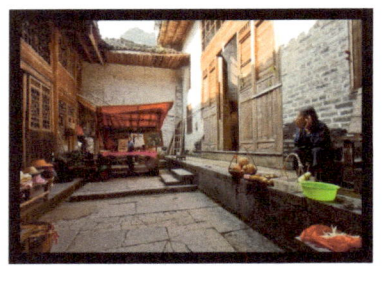

FISHING VILLAGE

12. follow this path
    然后沿着路往前走

13. follow the road down
    接着沿着路下坡

14. follow the road down
    继续下坡

15. follow the road down
    再下坡

16. viewpoint at your right
    这时你会看到如此图的景观

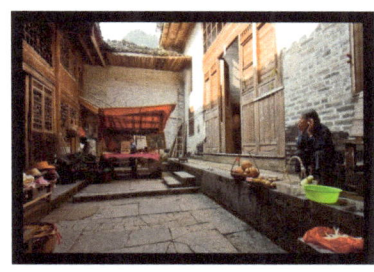

FISHING
VILLAGE

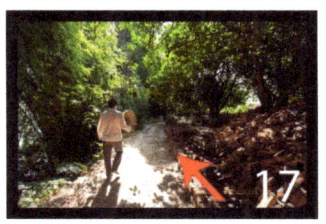

17

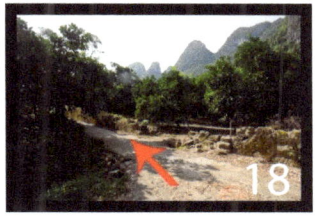

18

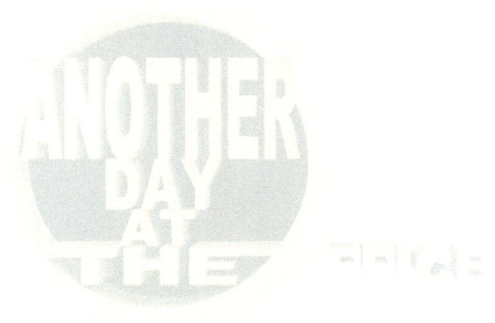

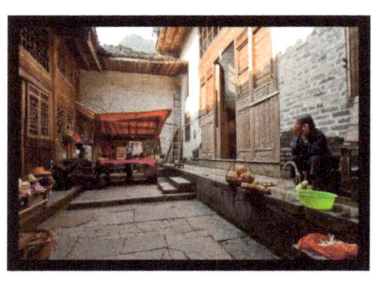

FISHING VILLAGE

17. follow the way,next to the river
沿着河边的这条小路往前走

18. after the intersection,go left
走到分叉路口时左转往
再走一段就到渔村了

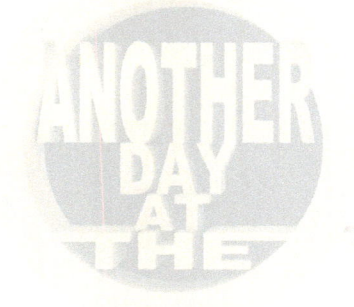

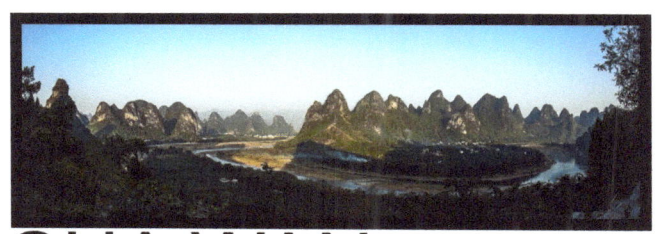

SHA WAN

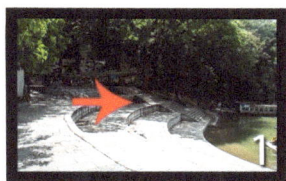

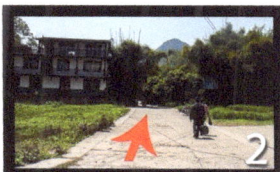

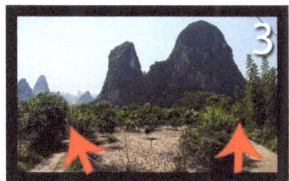

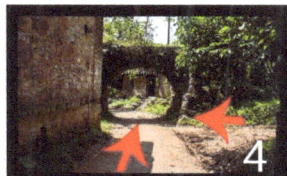

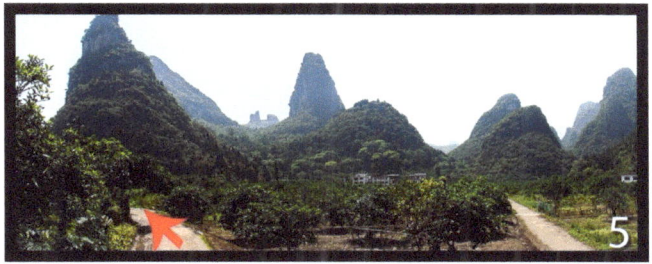

24

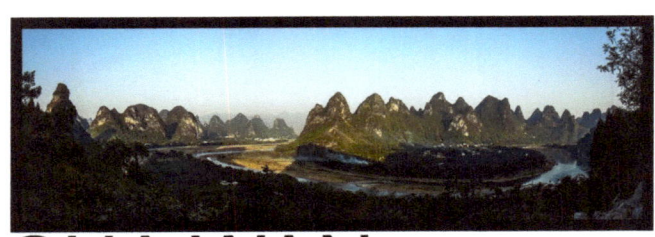

SHA WAN

1. take the ferry,across the river
   搭乘渡船过河

2. follow this path straight
   沿着这条路直走

3. you can take both paths
   这两条路都行得通

4. go under the bridge and follow untill this intersection
   穿过这座小拱门后继续往前走

5. at the intersection,go left
   到了这个岔路口则需要左转

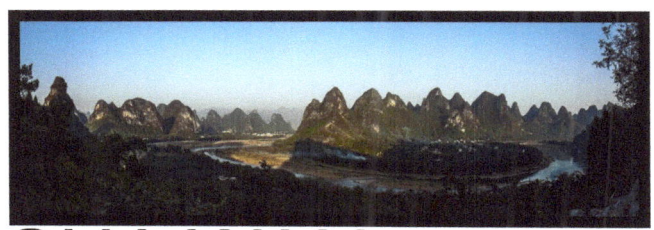

SHA WAN

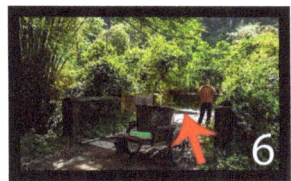

6

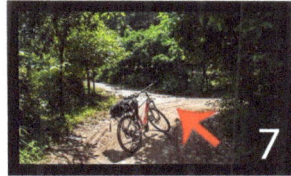

7

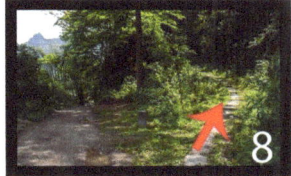

8

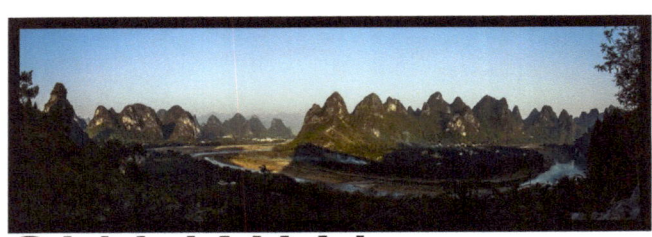

SHA WAN

6. pass the bridge and then turn left
   过了这座桥后左转

7. follow the path and then go left again
   沿河小路往前走到此路口，再左转

8. follow the path and at your right there's a stone path up
   继续前行，然后会看到
   右边一条小石板路蜿蜒上山

27

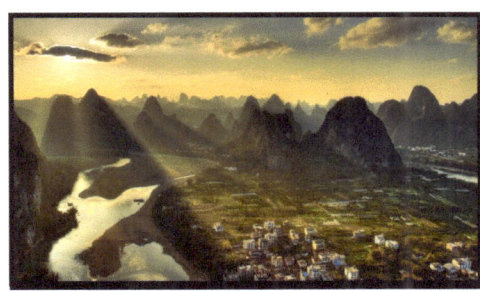

LAO-ZHAI HILL

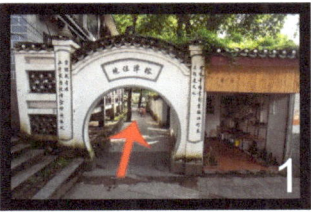

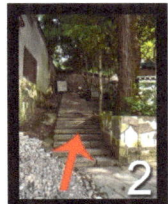

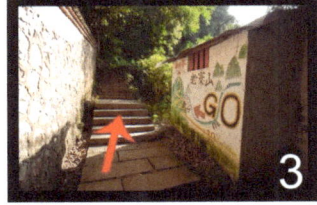

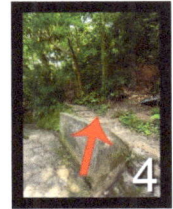

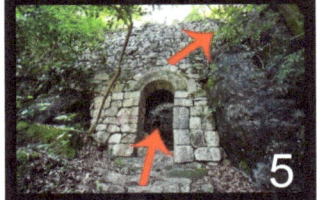

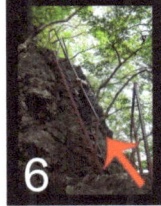

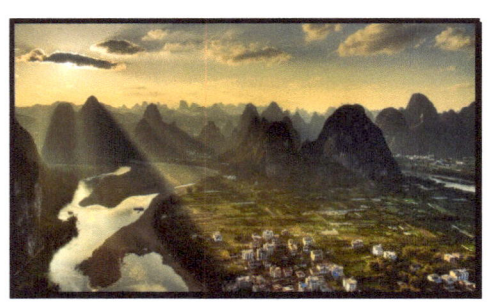

LAO-ZHAI HILL

1. walk to the big gate,at the left there's a white arch
   走到大牌坊的左侧会看到一个白拱门

2. enter,untill at your left steps go up,walk up
   过了拱门后直走至左手边有一条上山的小石板路

3. follow these steps up
   沿着石板路往上走

4. untill at your left theres another path up
   一直走到看见左手边有另一条小路上山

5. go through the gate and follow the arrows
   沿着小路上山，穿过一座石拱门之后沿着红色箭头继续上山

6. climb up this ladder and follow this path
   爬上铁梯子后往前走

29

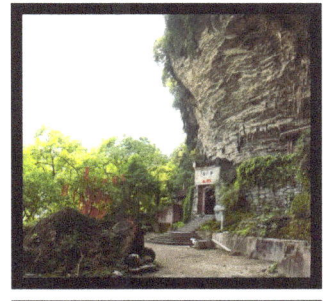

TENGJIAO
NUNNERY

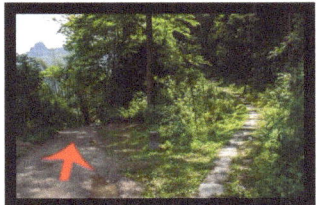

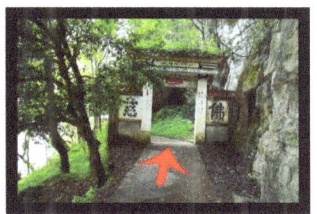

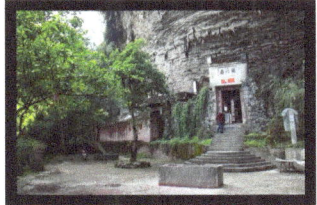

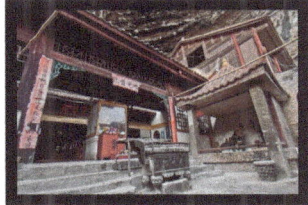

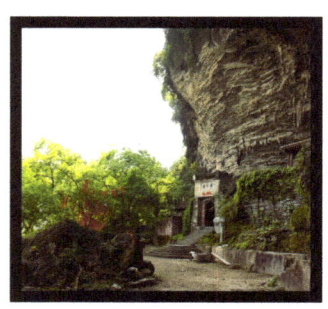

TENGJIAO NUNNERY

1. same direction as shawan,
but go left,where you go right for shawan
前面和去沙湾是一个方向，但是需要在此路口右转

2. follow this path and go through the gate
沿着小路往前走，穿过此门后即见腾蛟庵

31

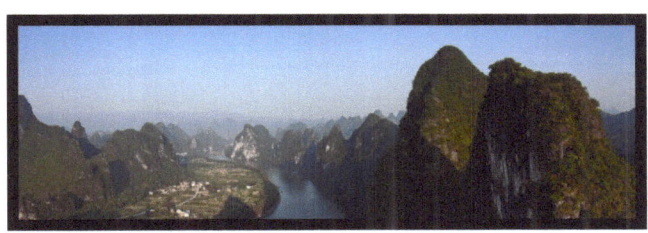

XIANGGONG .MAP p15f

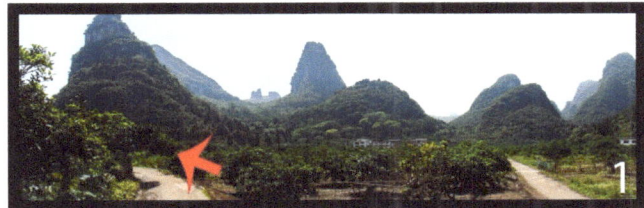

1

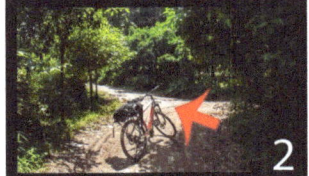

2

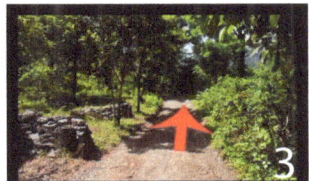

3

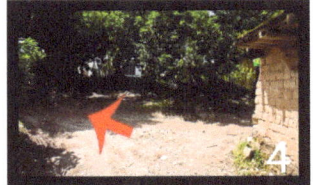

4

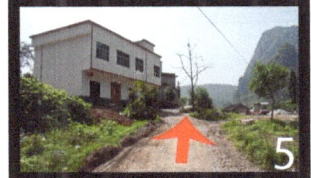

5

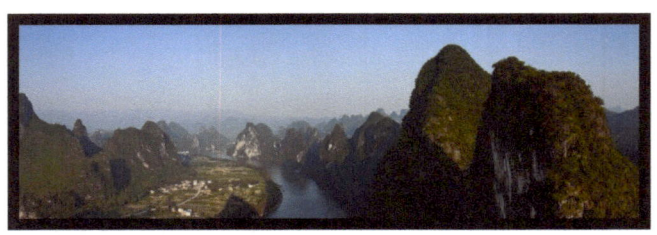

XIANGGONG

1. follow the same way as shawan
   请先根据去沙湾的路线一直走到此路口

2. turn left but at the next intersection turn right
   在此同样左转，但是到了下一个路口需要右转上山

3. follow this path,untill the clay house at your right
   沿此路前行直到看见这座土房子

4. at the clay house,turn left
   在土房子旁边的小路口左转

5. follow the path up and go straight
   继续前行，一直往前走

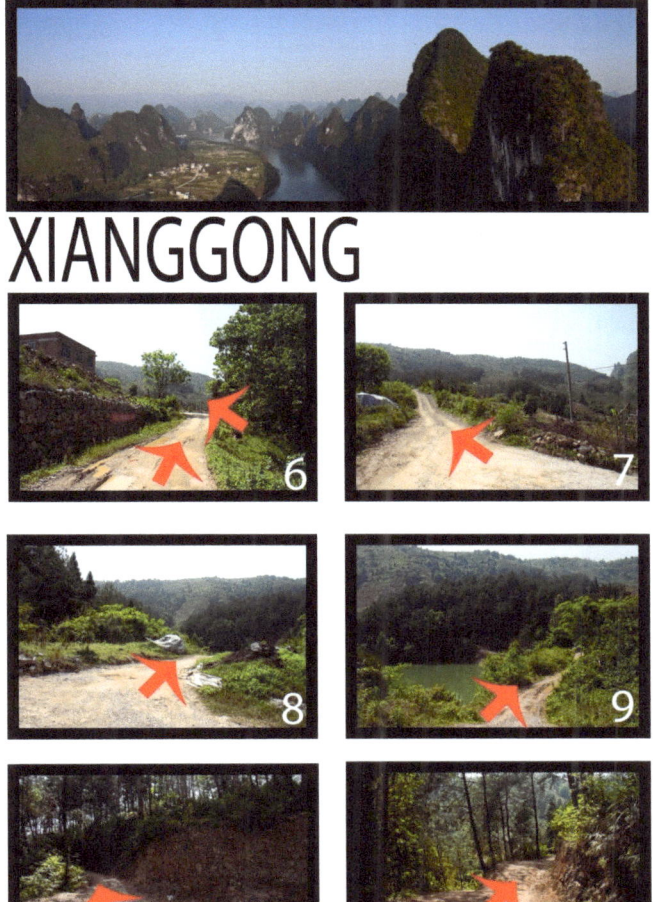

XIANGGONG

34

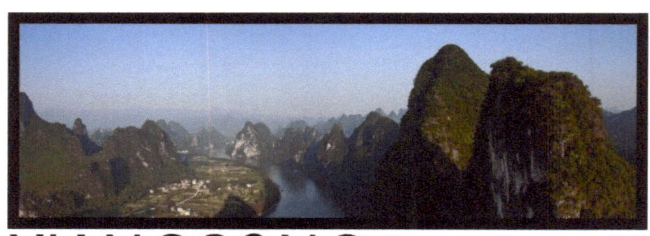

XIANGGONG

6. follow this path up and turn left
沿着这条路上山，然后左转

7. follow this path up
继续上山

8. untill at your right theres a path going down
然后你会看见路的右边有条小径走下坡

9. take the path down
沿着小径下坡

10. take left at the intersection
到这个分叉口后左转

11. follow the path ,that goes up the hill,at your right
之后又会看到右手边有小路可以上山

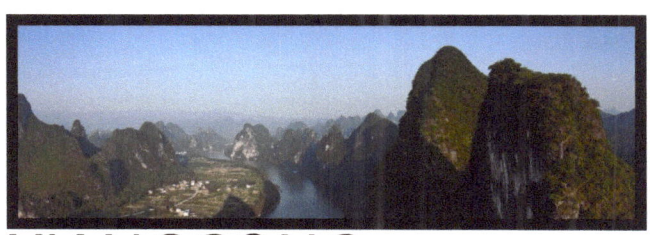

XIANGGONG

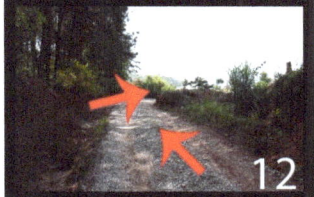

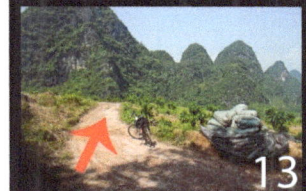

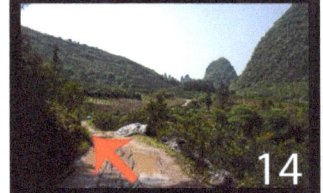

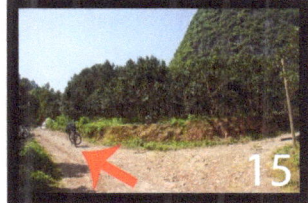

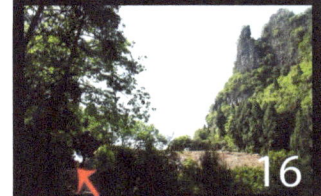

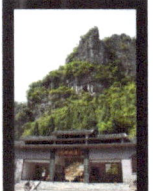

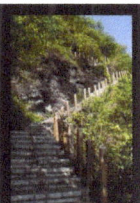

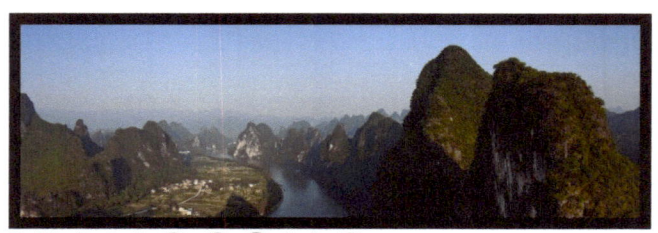

XIANGGONG

12. follow the path up and turn right

沿着小路上山，然后右转

13. follow the path at your right side

接着走右手边的这条路

14. follow the path up

沿着此路往山上走

15. follow the path up at your left

到此则需要走左手边的这条小路

16. follow the path up and there's your destination

继续前行一段时间后就
可以看到相公山了。

37

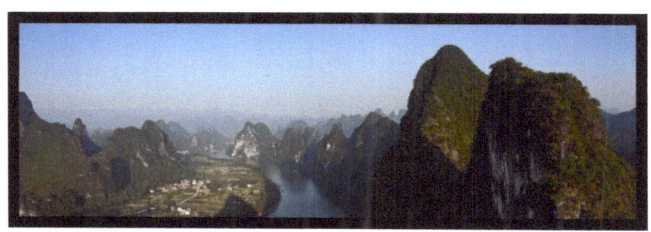

XIANGGONG way back

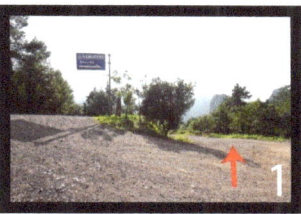
1

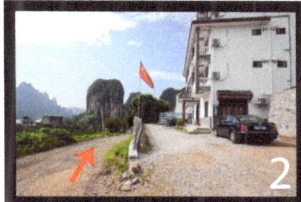
2

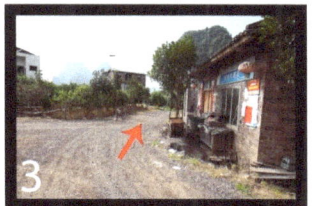
3

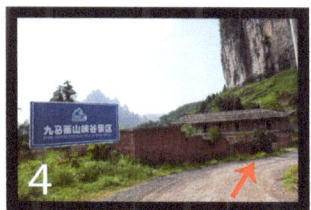
4

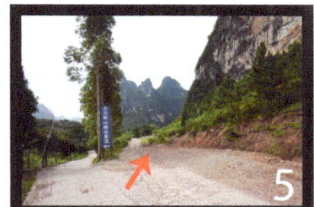
5

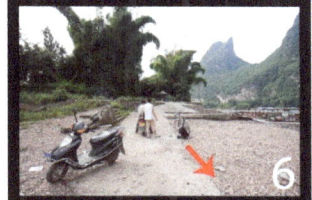
6

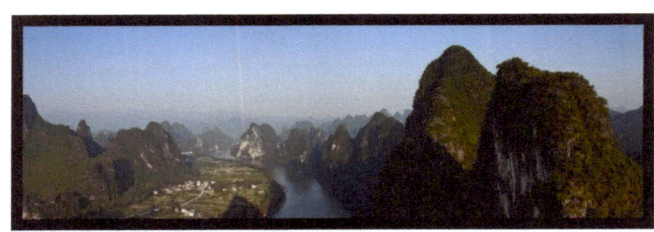

XIANGGONG way back

1. turn right to get back to xingping
在此右转可回兴坪

2. follow the path down to xingping at your left
沿着这条路前行

3. turn right at this intersection
在此路口右转

4. follow this path down
接续前行

5. follow the path at your right
在此走右手边这条路

6. follow the path down and cross the river and follow the road straight back to xingping
一直往下走，待过了河后沿着水泥路一直走到头就是兴坪镇

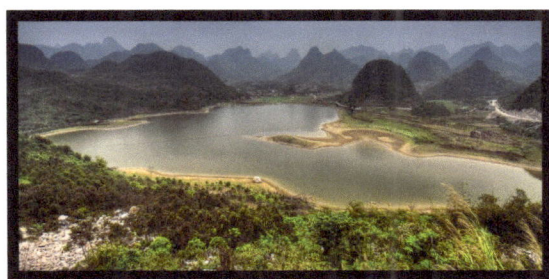

40

XITANG

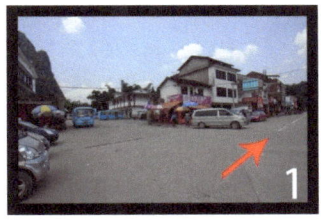

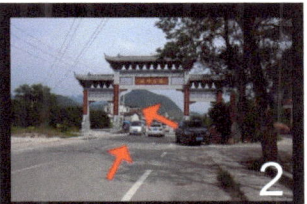

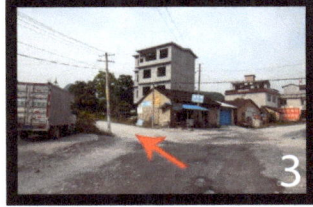

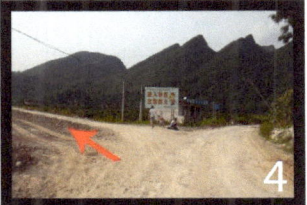

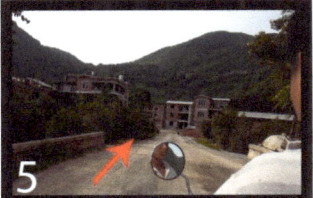

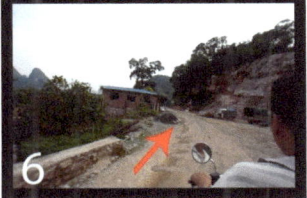

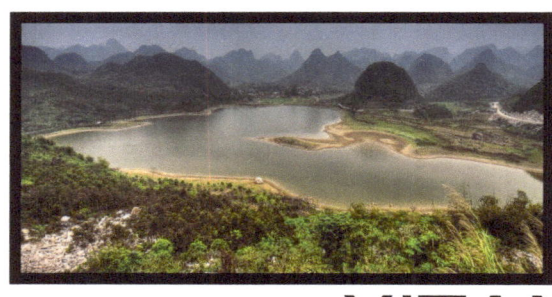

41

XITANG

1. turn right at xingping bus station and follow the road to yangshuo
出了汽车站后先沿着去阳朔的大路走一段

2. pass the gate and turn left and follow

3. follow the road,untill the next village and turn left there
前行至书家堡村，在村子的大路口处左转

4. follow the road for a while ,at this intersection turn left
继续前行至此路口，这里需要左转

5. pass through this little village
穿过这个小村子

6. follow the path and go up the hill
沿着此路前行，然后开始上山

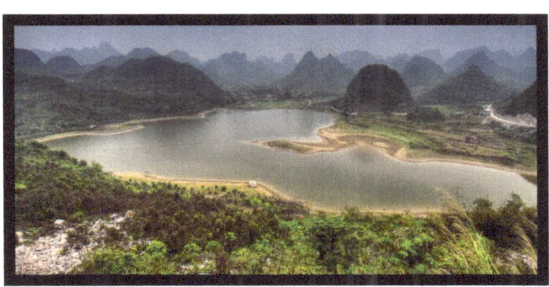

42

XITANG

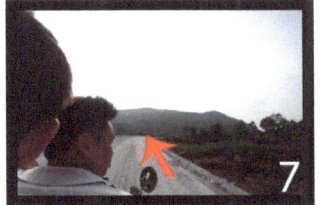

7

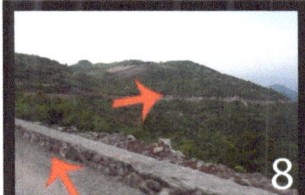

8

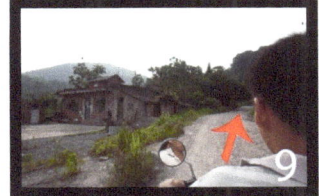

9

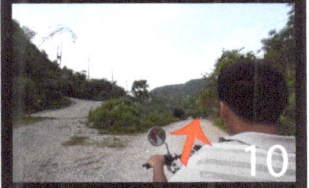

10

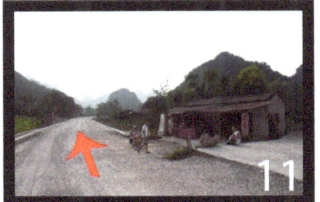

11

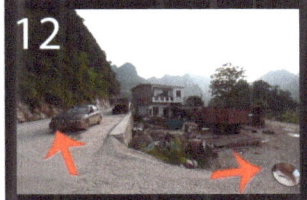

12

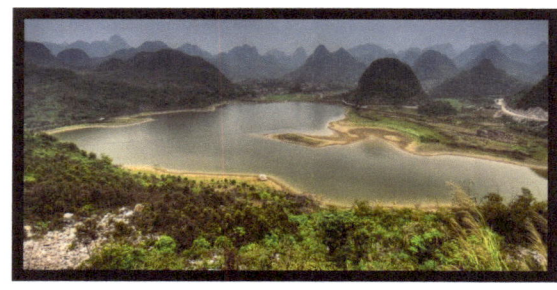

43

XITANG

7. follow this way up
沿此路上山

8. follow this road straight for a while
继续前行

9. follow this way up
接着沿此路上山

10. follow this way to your right
注意，在此要沿着右边的路直走

11. follow this way down,untill at your right
theres a little local shop
继续前行，然后会看到右边有这么个小商店

12. follow this way up or turn right
and you will see xitang lake
到这里就是西塘水库了，
可以前行走到山腰俯瞰湖面，也可以
右转走到湖边

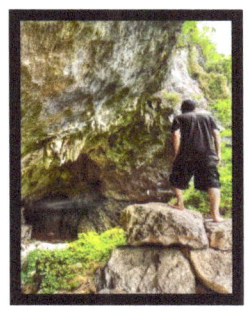

HIDDEN CAVE

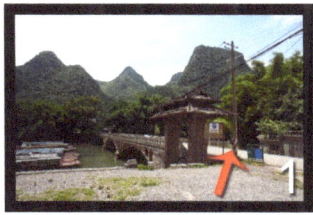
1

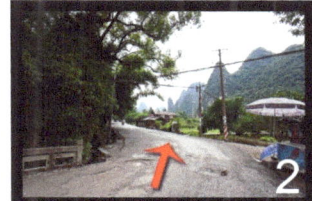
2

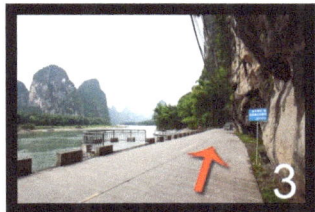
3

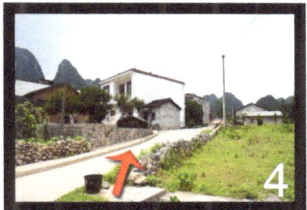
4

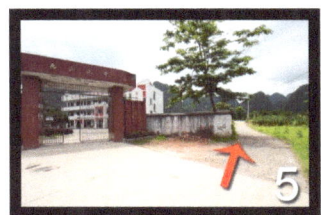
5

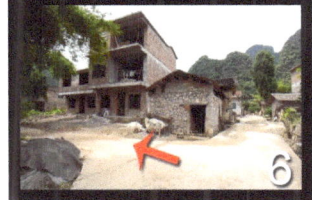
6

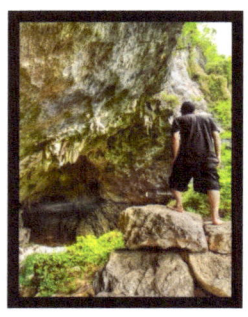

HIDDEN CAVE

1. cross the bridge
过了这座桥

2. turn left and follow the road
左转沿着路往前走

3. keep following the road
一直往前走

4. at your right,follow the road to a school
此时需右转走到这座希望小学旁边

5. take the path at right,follow it
走小学右边的小路，一直往前走

6. untill these houses,turn left
看到这些房子的时候左转

45

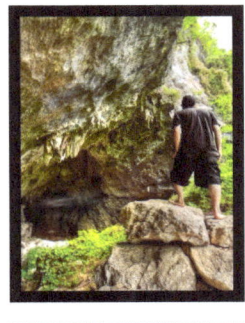

HIDDEN
CAVE

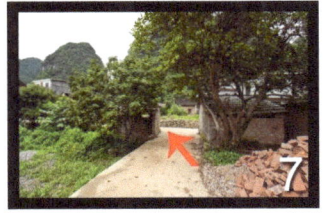
7

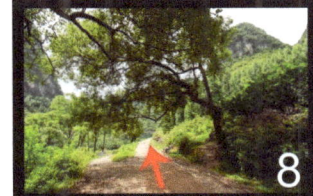
8

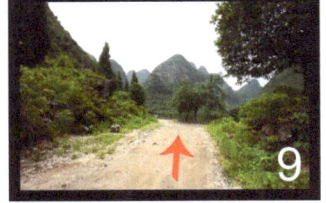
9

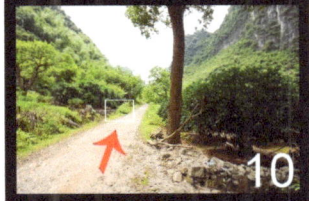
10

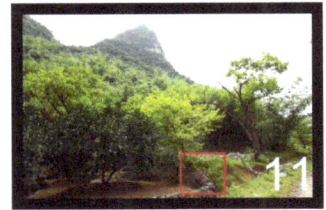
11

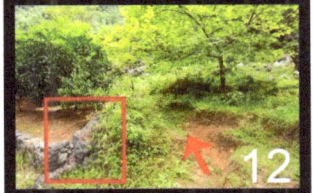
12

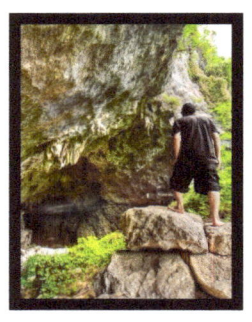

HIDDEN CAVE

7. follow the path untill the intersection,then turn left
往前走到这个路口时左转

8. follow the dirt path up the hill
接下来要沿着土路上山

9. downhill from there,follow the path
上到顶后又要下坡，继续前行

10. untill at your left,theres a stone fence
直到看见左手边有一排矮石墙

11. at the end of this fence,theres a red marking
在石墙末端漆有个红色标志

12. follow this red marking up
在红色标志这里左转

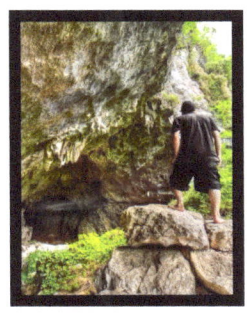

HIDDEN
CAVE

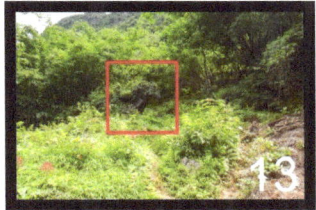

13

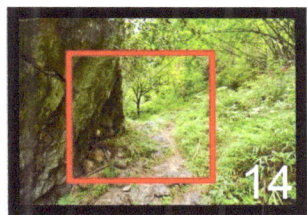

14

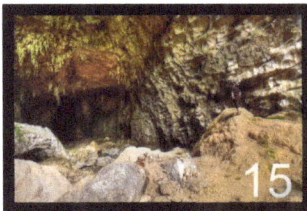

15

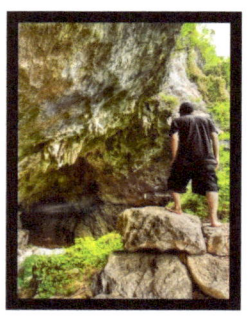

HIDDEN CAVE

13. follow the path to the overhanging rock
往前走会看到一块突出的大石块

14. pass the overhanging rock
需要走过个石块

15. follow this path ,untill you get at the cave
继续沿着小路走，转几弯就会
走到洞口了

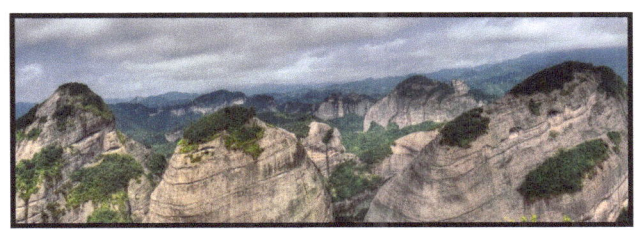

BAJIAOZHAI/EIGHT ANGLE
NORTHEAST OF GUILIN ON THE BORDER WITH HUNAN

1. NOT THE EASIEST PLACE TO GET TO
   GET A BUS FROM GUILIN BUS STATION
   TO ZIYUAN

2. CROSS THE CITY BY LOCAL BIKE
   TO GET THE LOCAL BUS TO MEIXI

3. SPEND THE NIGHT THERE OR GET A LOCAL BIKE
   TO GET YOU TO THE ENTRANCE OF THE PARK

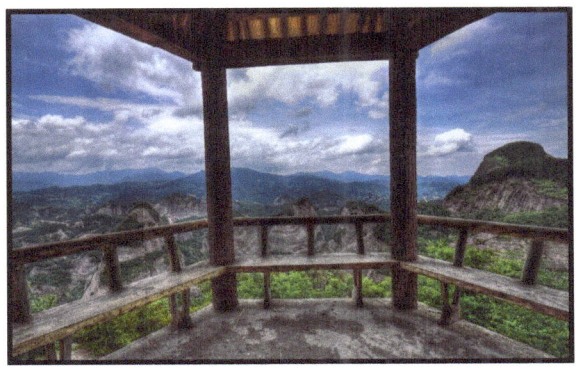

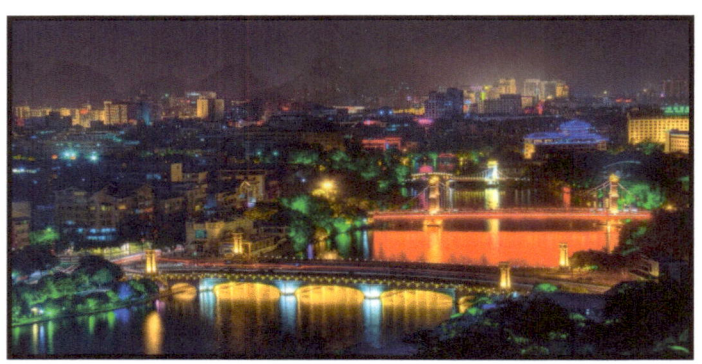

THE CITY OF GUILIN

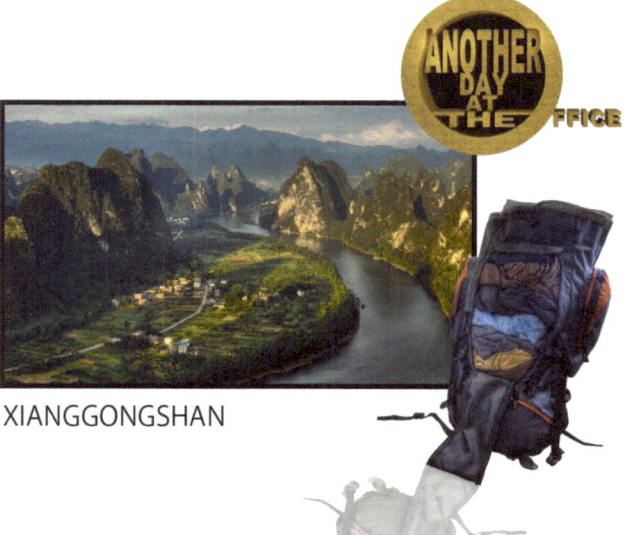

XIANGGONGSHAN

WWW.ANOTHERDAYATTHEOFFICE.ORG